LIFE PICTURE PUZZLE

WELCOME TO LIFE'S SEVENTH PICTURE PUZZLE BOOK

There are good reasons why people across the world get together with friends and family during the darkest and coldest days of winter. Christmas, Kwanzaa, Hanukkah and the other holidays that people honor all celebrate certain common themes—the friendship and love that bind families together, the need for sustaining communities during hard times, and, in the depths of winter, the promise of a renewal of life, of the spring to come.

Those universal traditions convinced our team at LIFE that the winter holidays should be the theme for our next Picture Puzzle book. We wanted to give our readers a book to cuddle up with, something they could share with their families during cold and blustery nights best spent indoors. So our photo editors began their search once again, this time hunting for touching and amusing photographs of holiday celebrations worldwide. Then, we set our mad Puzzle Master loose to craft the kind of engaging and confounding puzzles he is best at. Although it was the height of summer for us, we had a lot of fun imagining a winter wonderland, and we hope we can share some of our good times with you. We've included some homey Thanksgiving and exciting New Year's pictures as well.

Everything you know and love about our puzzle books is still here. The Novice section is meant for our first-time readers, with amusing puzzles that won't frustrate you—too much. The difficulty of our puzzles increases slowly throughout our Master and Expert sections until you reach our Genius puzzles, which are meant to tease and provoke you with their complexity. And it wouldn't be a LIFE Picture Puzzle book without our Classics section, which features wonderful black-and-white photography from LIFE's historic photo archive.

We're already talking about our next Picture Puzzle book. The theme is still a secret—even we aren't sure what it is. You can make suggestions yourself, and let us know what you think of our Holidays book at picturepuzzle@life.com.

Keep those e-mails coming!

[OUR CUT-UP PUZZLES: EASY AS 1-2-3]

We scissored a photo into 4 to 9 pieces. Then we rearranged the pieces and numbered them.

Your mission: Beneath each cut-up puzzle, write the number of the piece in the box where it belongs.

Check the answer key at the back of the book to see what the reassembled image looks like.

[HOW TO PLAY THE PUZZLES]

A Night of Miracles

In this case, sincerity trumps acting skills

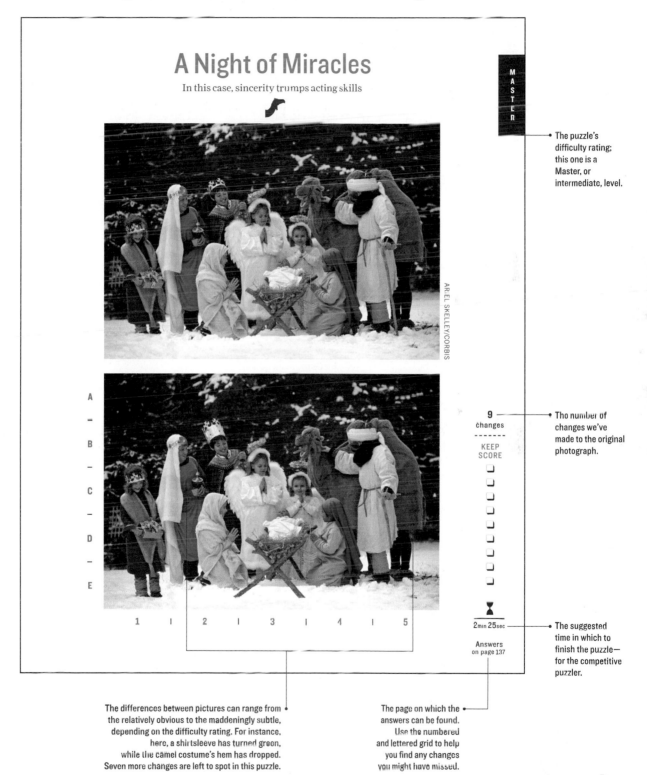

AR EL SKELLEY/CORBIS

The puzzle's difficulty rating; this one is a Master, or intermediate, level.

9
changes
- - - - - -
KEEP
SCORE

2min 25sec

Answers
on page 137

The number of changes we've made to the original photograph.

The suggested time in which to finish the puzzle—for the competitive puzzler.

The differences between pictures can range from the relatively obvious to the maddeningly subtle, depending on the difficulty rating. For instance, here, a shirtsleeve has turned green, while the camel costume's hem has dropped. Seven more changes are left to spot in this puzzle.

The page on which the answers can be found. Use the numbered and lettered grid to help you find any changes you might have missed.

LIFE PICTURE PUZZLE

Puzzle Master Michael Roseman
Editor Robert Sullivan
Director of Photography Barbara Baker Burrows
Deputy Picture Editor Christina Lieberman
Copy Barbara Gogan (Chief), Heather L. Hughes
Research Editor Marilyn Fu
Photo Assistant Forrester Hambrecht

LIFE Puzzle Books
Managing Editor Bill Shapiro

LIFE Books
President Andrew Blau
Business Manager Roger Adler
Business Development Manager Jeff Burak

Editorial Operations
Richard K. Prue, David Sloan (Directors), Richard Shaffer (Group Manager),
Brian Fellows, Raphael Joa, Angel Mass, Stanley E. Moyse, Albert Rufino (Managers),
Soheila Asayesh, Keith Aurelio, Trang Ba Chuong, Charlotte Coco, Osmar Escalona,
Kevin Hart, Norma Jones, Mert Kerimoglu, Rosalie Khan, Marco Lau, Po Fung Ng,
Rudi Papiri, Barry Pribula, Carina A. Rosario, Christopher Scala, Diana Suryakusuma,
Vaune Trachtman, Paul Tupay, Lionel Vargas, David Weiner

Time Inc. Home Entertainment
Publisher Richard Fraiman
General Manager Steven Sandonato
Executive Director, Marketing Services Carol Pittard
Director, Retail & Special Sales Tom Mifsud
Director, New Product Development Peter Harper
Assistant Director, Newsstand Marketing Laura Adam
Assistant Director, Brand Marketing Joy Butts
Associate Counsel Helen Wan
Senior Brand Manager, TWRS/M Holly Oakes
Book Production Manager Suzanne Janso
Design & Prepress Manager Anne-Michelle Gallero
Brand Manager Shelley Rescober

Special thanks to Glenn Buonocore, Susan Chodakiewicz, Margaret Hess,
Brynn Joyce, Robert Marasco, Brooke Reger, Mary Sarro-Waite, Ilene Schreider,
Adriana Tierno, Alex Voznesenskiy

PUBLISHED BY

LIFE Books

Vol. 8, No. 10 • October 20, 2008

Copyright 2008
Time Inc.
1271 Avenue of the Americas
New York, New York 10020

We welcome your comments and suggestions about LIFE Books. Please write to us at:
LIFE Books
Attention: Book Editors
PO Box 11016
Des Moines, IA 50336-1016

If you would like to order any of our hardcover Collector's Edition books, please call us at 1-800-327-6388
(Monday through Friday, 7 a.m. to 8 p.m., or Saturday, 7 a.m. to 6 p.m. Central Time).

READY, SET, GO!

These puzzles are for everyone:
rookies and veterans,
young and old. Start here, and
sharpen your skills.

Elf Incoming

How else do you think the presents get there on time?

A
—
B
—
C
—
D
—
E

1   2   3   4   5

7
changes

⧗
1min 40sec

Answers
on page 137

KEEP SCORE ★ ❏ ❏ ❏ ❏ ❏ ❏ ❏

Ring Around the Snowman

Judging by his frown, the spring thaw must be near

A
B
C
D
E

1   2   3   4   5

9
changes
- - - - - - - - -
KEEP
SCORE

❏
❏
❏
❏
❏
❏
❏
❏
❏

⏳

2min 5sec

Answers
on page 137

The Scent of Winter

This big guy can tell hard times are coming

A
–
B
–
C
–
D
–
E

1   2   3   4   5

8
changes

2min 20sec

Answers
on page 137

KEEP SCORE ★ ❑ ❑ ❑ ❑ ❑ ❑ ❑ ❑

Fire Down Under

In Sydney, the New Year comes in with short sleeves *and* the rockets' red glare

STEVE ALLEN/GETTY

A

B

C

D

E

1 | 2 | 3 | 4 | 5

6
changes
- - - - - - - - -
KEEP
SCORE
❑
❑
❑
❑
❑
❑

⧗
1min 55sec

Answers
on page 137

Ho! Ho! Aloha!

Mele Kalikimaka to you and yours

7
changes

⧗

2min 40sec

Answers
on page 137

KEEP SCORE ★ ❏ ❏ ❏ ❏ ❏ ❏ ❏

Hay There!

First bring in the harvest, then give thanks

A

B

C

D

E

1   2   3   4   5

6
changes

⧖

2min 10sec

Answers
on page 137

KEEP SCORE ★ ❑ ❑ ❑ ❑ ❑ ❑

Pining for Christmas

Even the horses are wearing their finest

A

B

C

D

E

1　　2　　3　　4　　5

6
changes

⏳
1min 40sec

Answers
on page 137

KEEP SCORE ★ ❏ ❏ ❏ ❏ ❏ ❏

North Pole Pooches

They're part of Santa's K-9 auxiliary

MARGO SILVER/GETTY

8
changes

- - - - - - - - -

KEEP
SCORE

❑
❑
❑
❑
❑
❑
❑
❑

⏳

2min 45sec

Answers
on page 137

A

B

C

D

E

1   2   3   4   5

On Holiday

Kicking back during Christmas break

A
—
B
—
C
—
D
—
E

1   2   3   4   5

7
changes

- - - - - - - -
KEEP
SCORE

☐
☐
☐
☐
☐
☐

2min 25sec

Answers
on page 137

Santa's Not-So-Little Helpers

Talk about your Polar Express!

✈

9
changes

- - - - - - - - -

KEEP
SCORE

❑
❑
❑
❑
❑
❑
❑
❑
❑

⧗

2min 55sec

Answers
on page 137

Silent Night

All is calm, all is bright

FRIDMAR DAMM/CORBIS

A
B
C
D
E

1   2   3   4   5

9
changes

⧗

3min 15sec

Answers
on page 138

KEEP SCORE ★ ❑ ❑ ❑ ❑ ❑ ❑ ❑ ❑ ❑

Looking for a Hiding Place

Turkey Day's coming, and they're getting going

JOE MCDONALD/CORBIS

7
changes

- - - - - - - - -

KEEP
SCORE

☐
☐
☐
☐
☐
☐
☐

⧖

3min 5sec

Answers
on page 138

A
—
B
—
C
—
D
—
E

1   2   3   4   5

A Wish and a Prayer

Everyone lights candles during the holidays

MARK ADAMS/GETTY

9
changes

KEEP
SCORE

3min 35sec

Answers
on page 138

Rock Center Serenade

Can you guess how many lightbulbs the famous Rockefeller Center tree needs?
Did someone say 30,000?

MIKE SEGAR/CORBIS

A
—
B
—
C
—
D
—
E

1   2   3   4   5

8
changes

⏳
3min 45sec

Answers
on page 138

KEEP SCORE ★ ❑ ❑ ❑ ❑ ❑ ❑ ❑ ❑

Fan-tastic Festivities

New Year's Day comes to Okinawa with pomp and circumstance

HITOSHI MAESHIRO/CORBIS

A

B

C

D

E

1   2   3   4   5

8
changes

- - - - - - - - -

KEEP
SCORE

❏
❏
❏
❏
❏
❏
❏
❏

⧖

3min 55sec

Answers
on page 138

Winter Wonderland

Don't let us snow you with this one

1

2

3

4

5

6

0min 15sec

Answer
on page 138

NICOLA ANGELI/CORBIS

Wet Christmas

Gurgle all the waaay!

1

2

3

4

5

MILUTIN SEKULOVSKI/GETTY

6

0min 35sec

Answer
on page 138

Northward Ho!

A big thrill for these skiers on the big night

MICHAEL DEYOUNG/CORBIS

5   4   3   2   1

A   B   C   D   E

8
changes

- - - - - - - - -

KEEP
SCORE

⌛

3min 15sec

Answers
on page 138

Slippin' and Slidin'

Setting sail for a brand-new year

A
B
C
D
E

1   2   3   4   5

10
changes

4min 10sec

Answers
on page 138

KEEP SCORE ★ ❑ ❑ ❑ ❑ ❑ ❑ ❑ ❑ ❑ ❑

New Year's Wishes

Help them put their season's greetings in order

NOBORU HASHIMOTO/CORBIS

0min 25sec

Answer
on page 138

KEEP SCORE

Cold War

Move the pieces in this battle between East and West

SEAN MCKAY/GETTY

KEEP SCORE

0min 30sec

Answer
on page 138

Brought to You by the Letter *B*

What's big and yellow and lighter than air?

PETER FOLEY/CORBIS

5 | 4 | 3 | 2 | 1

A | B | C | D | E

9
changes

- - - - - - - - -

KEEP
SCORE

4min 5sec

Answers
on page 138

ERL 1

Here, puzzles get
a little harder. You'll
need to raise
your game a level.

Riding the Rails

Santa's changed his commute so he can catch up on his reading

TONY LEWIS/GETTY

A
B
C
D
E

1   2   3   4   5

9 changes

3min 35sec

Answers on page 139

KEEP SCORE ★ ☐ ☐ ☐ ☐ ☐ ☐ ☐ ☐ ☐

Apple Pie-to-Be

Just add a scoop of vanilla ice cream
and give thanks to Johnny Appleseed

HANS REINHARD/CORBIS

A

B

C

D

E

1   2   3   4   5

7
changes

⏳
3min 45sec

Answers
on page 139

KEEP SCORE ★ ☐ ☐ ☐ ☐ ☐ ☐ ☐

Who Let the Hounds Out?

Boxing Day comes to England with a bark and a howl

1min 10sec

Answer
on page 139

STEPHEN ROMILLY/CORBIS

Let Sleeping Bears Lie

We dare you to take his gifts away from him

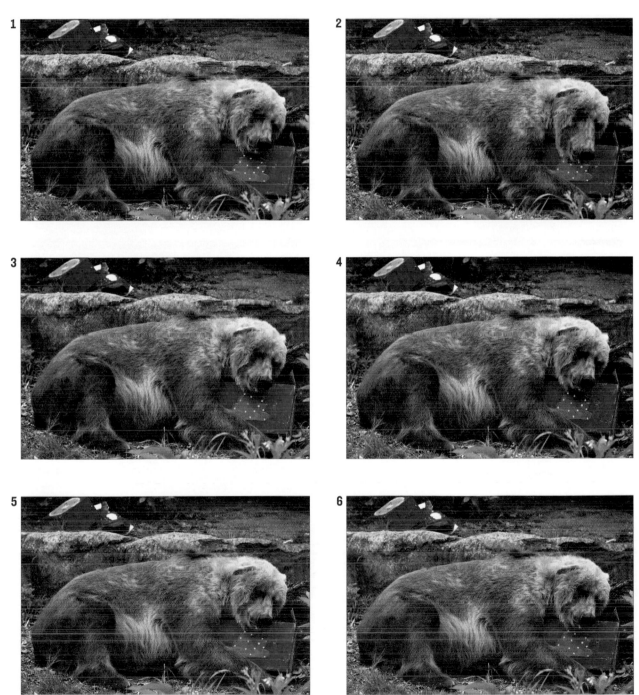

LISA MAREE WILLIAMS/GETTY

1min 40sec

Answer
on page 139

The Holidays Make Us Sappy
Sweet treats are made from these

JONATHAN BLAIR/CORBIS

A
—
B
—
C
—
D
—
E

1   2   3   4   5

9
changes

⏳
4min 10sec

Answers
on page 139

KEEP SCORE ★ ☐ ☐ ☐ ☐ ☐ ☐ ☐ ☐ ☐ ☐

Window-Shopping

This officer is at liberty to take in the sights

MATTHEW PEYTON/GETTY

A
—
B
—
C
—
D
—
E

1 | 2 | 3 | 4 | 5

Capital Decorations

It's the stars and stripes forever

GREG PEASE/GETTY

A

—

B

—

C

—

D

—

E

1   2   3   4   5

8
changes
- - - - - - - - -
KEEP
SCORE

❏
❏
❏
❏
❏
❏
❏
❏

⌛

4min 5sec

Answers
on page 139

Everything Old Is New Again

How thankful are they?
Hard to tell.

A

—

B

—

C

—

D

—

E

1 | 2 | 3 | 4 | 5

7
changes

⧗
3min 25sec

Answers
on page 139

KEEP SCORE ★ ❏ ❏ ❏ ❏ ❏ ❏ ❏

Baby, It's Cold Outside

Dreaming of a white Christmas, or a warm hearth?

ESCHCOLLECTION/GETTY

A — B — C — D — E

1 | 2 | 3 | 4 | 5

10 changes

⏳

4min 50sec

Answers on page 139

KEEP SCORE ★ ❏ ❏ ❏ ❏ ❏ ❏ ❏ ❏ ❏ ❏

Sleigh to Go

And they're laughing all the way

A

—

B

—

C

—

D

—

E

1 | 2 | 3 | 4 | 5

12
changes

⏳

4min 20sec

Answers
on page 139

KEEP SCORE ★ ☐ ☐ ☐ ☐ ☐ ☐ ☐ ☐ ☐ ☐ ☐ ☐

Auld Lang Syne

Rocket science at its most beautiful

8
changes

3min 35sec

Answers
on page 139

KEEP SCORE ★ ❏ ❏ ❏ ❏ ❏ ❏ ❏ ❏

Early to Rise

Now that he's up, he has to play the waiting game

A

B

C

D

E

1   2   3   4   5

11
changoc
- - - - - - - - -
KEEP
SCORE

☐
☐
☐
☐
☐
☐
☐
☐
☐
☐

⌛

3min 55sec

Answers
on page 140

Camel Rides: Only One Ruble

Grandfather Frost and Snow Girl grin as they flee Mother Winter's embrace

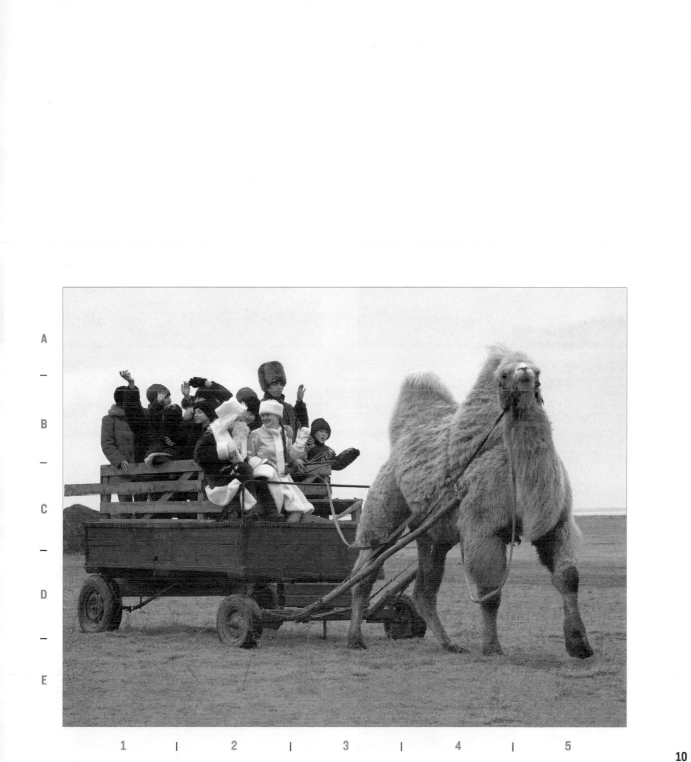

A
—
B
—
C
—
D
—
E

1 | 2 | 3 | 4 | 5

10
changes

⧗
3min 35sec

Answers
on page 140

KEEP SCORE ★ ☐ ☐ ☐ ☐ ☐ ☐ ☐ ☐ ☐ ☐

The Russians Are Coming

Five are just the same. Which picture isn't?

1

2

3

4

5

6

1min 15sec

Answer
on page 140

GARETH CATTERMOLE/GETTY

Fa-La-La-La-La!

One choir's a little quirky

1

2

3

4

5

RUDY SULGAN/CORBIS

6

1min 45sec

Answer
on page 140

Dancing for Snowflakes

These girls have high hopes as they sway their way into Christmas

DOUGLAS PEEBLES/CORBIS

A

B

C

D

E

1 | 2 | 3 | 4 | 5

12
changes

⧗

4min 40sec

Answers
on page 140

KEEP SCORE ★ ☐ ☐ ☐ ☐ ☐ ☐ ☐ ☐ ☐ ☐ ☐ ☐

It's a Wrap

Looks like Santa stopped here more than once

LEW ROBERTSON/CORBIS

A
—
B
—
C
—
D
—
E

1   2   3   4   5

11
changes
- - - - - - - -
KEEP
SCORE

⌛
4min 35sec

Answers
on page 140

Monkey Shines

It's New Year's in Singapore and he's dancing it in with style

A
–
B
–
C
–
D
–
E

1   2   3   4   5

12
changes

⧗

4min 15sec

Answers
on page 140

KEEP SCORE ★ ☐ ☐ ☐ ☐ ☐ ☐ ☐ ☐ ☐ ☐ ☐ ☐

Central Cooling

This ice palace needs a redesign

1min 15sec

Answer
on page 140

KEEP SCORE

The Brothers Claus

These Santas need a little help.
Can you give them a push in the right direction?

KEEP SCORE

55sec

Answer
on page 140

All Tied Down

The webcrawler gets a taste of his own medicine

DAVID KATZENSTEIN/CORBIS

5

4

3

2

1

A

B

C

D

E

10
changes

KEEP
SCORE

❏
❏
❏
❏
❏
❏
❏
❏
❏
❏

⏳
4min 45sec

Answers
on page 140

RT[ ]

Only serious puzzlers
dare to tread past this point.
Who's in?

The Glow of the Season
The snow provides a lovely accent

A

B

C

D

E

1   2   3   4   5

12
changes

⧗

5min 5sec

Answers
on page 140

KEEP SCORE ★ ❑ ❑ ❑ ❑ ❑ ❑ ❑ ❑ ❑ ❑ ❑ ❑

Caught Napping

Somebody woke up just in the nick of time

A
B
C
D
E

1   2   3   4   5

14
changes

⏳

5min 25sec

Answers
on page 141

KEEP SCORE ★ ☐ ☐ ☐ ☐ ☐ ☐ ☐ ☐ ☐ ☐ ☐ ☐ ☐ ☐

A Bumpkin With Pumpkins

After we make jack-o'-lanterns, we'll bake pies

A

B

C

D

E

1   2   3   4   5

12
changes
- - - - - - - - -
KEEP
SCORE

☐
☐
☐
☐
☐
☐
☐
☐
☐
☐
☐
☐

⌛
5min 15sec

Answers
on page 141

Teach Your Children Well

Care to take a spin on this one?

STEPHANE LEHR/CORBIS

A
B
C
D
E

1   2   3   4   5

11
changes

⧖

4min 10sec

Answers
on page 141

KEEP SCORE ★ ☐ ☐ ☐ ☐ ☐ ☐ ☐ ☐ ☐ ☐ ☐

Dicey Business

The bear's too blasé to notice that these dice aren't nice

12
changes

KEEP
SCORE

☐
☐
☐
☐
☐
☐
☐
☐
☐
☐
☐
☐

⌛

5min 15sec

Answers
on page 141

That Lived-In Look

Christmas comes even to those without the Martha Stewart touch

K S MORTON/CORBIS

9
changes

- - - - - - - -

KEEP
SCORE

☐
☐
☐
☐
☐
☐
☐
☐
☐

⌛

4min 45sec

Answers
on page 141

A

B

C

D

E

1   2   3   4   5

Santa's Mail Room

All those letters and cards will keep them plenty busy

CAROLINE BLUMBERG/CORBIS

8
changes

KEEP
SCORE

4min 40sec

Answers
on page 141

Dive, Dive, Dive

Father Christmas travels by plane, train, automobile, sleigh . . . and sub

A

B

C

D

E

1   2   3   4   5

11
changes

KEEP
SCORE

⌛
4min 35sec

Answers
on page 141

In Search of Santa's Workshop

They may never know how close they are

LAYNE KENNEDY/CORBIS

A
—
B
—
C
—
D
—
E

1   2   3   4   5

10
changes

⧗

5min 25sec

Answers
on page 141

KEEP SCORE ★ ❏ ❏ ❏ ❏ ❏ ❏ ❏ ❏ ❏ ❏

The North Wind Blows

Corral the photo that's different before these ponies catch cold

1

2

3

4

5

6

2min 10sec

Answer
on page 141

JAMES GRITZ/GETTY

Berried Alive

What's a Thanksgiving table without cranberry sauce?

1

2

3

4

5

PHILIPPE BOURSEILLER/GETTY

6

1min 55sec

Answer
on page 141

Gabriel, Blow Your Horn!

Gabriel's the guy on the left

SANDRA RACCANELLO/CORBIS

12
changes

- - - - - - - -

KEEP
SCORE

5min 40sec

Answers
on page 141

A

—

B

—

C

—

D

—

E

1 | 2 | 3 | 4 | 5

Please Don't Eat the Houses

These little architects keep sampling their work

ARIEL SKELLEY/CORBIS

11
changes

KEEP
SCORE

5min 25sec

Answers
on page 142

It's Called Skijoring

And it's one way to get the blood flowing on a cold winter morning

ARNO BALZARINI/CORBIS

A   B   C   D   E

1   2   3   4   5

16
changes

- - - - - - - - -

KEEP
SCORE

❏ ❏ ❏ ❏ ❏ ❏ ❏ ❏ ❏ ❏ ❏ ❏ ❏ ❏ ❏ ❏

⧗

5min 55sec

Answers
on page 142

Finding a single difference in these puzzles is a challenge. Finding them all might be impossible.

Look! It's Sandy Claus!

He's here to catch the big one

A
—
B
—
C
—
D
—
E

1   2   3   4   5

14
changes

⧗

5min 10,000

Answers
on page 142

KEEP SCORE ★ ❏ ❏ ❏ ❏ ❏ ❏ ❏ ❏ ❏ ❏ ❏ ❏ ❏ ❏ ❏

Urban Snowscape

Sometimes nature makes you take the time to relax

KELLY RYERSON/GETTY

A
—
B
—
C
—
D
—
E

1 | 2 | 3 | 4 | 5

10
changes

KEEP
SCORE

❏
❏
❏
❏
❏
❏
❏
❏
❏
❏

⌛
5min 15sec

Answers
on page 142

Make Like a Nutcracker

Winter's stomping in with its big boots on

12
changes

KEEP
SCORE

⌛

5min 5sec

Answers
on page 142

A

B

C

D

E

1   2   3   4   5

GENIUS

Pudding

At least, that's what some call it

TREVOR WOOD/GETTY

13
changes

KEEP
SCORE

☐
☐
☐
☐
☐
☐
☐
☐
☐
☐
☐
☐
☐

⌛

5min 25sec

Answers
on page 142

Candle Power

Christmas at this home is off the grid

A
—
B
—
C
—
D
—
E

1   2   3   4   5

17
changes

6min 10sec

Answers
on page 142

KEEP SCORE ★ ❏ ❏ ❏ ❏ ❏ ❏ ❏ ❏ ❏ ❏ ❏ ❏ ❏ ❏ ❏ ❏ ❏

Frosty's Beauticians

This crew gets paid in cold cash

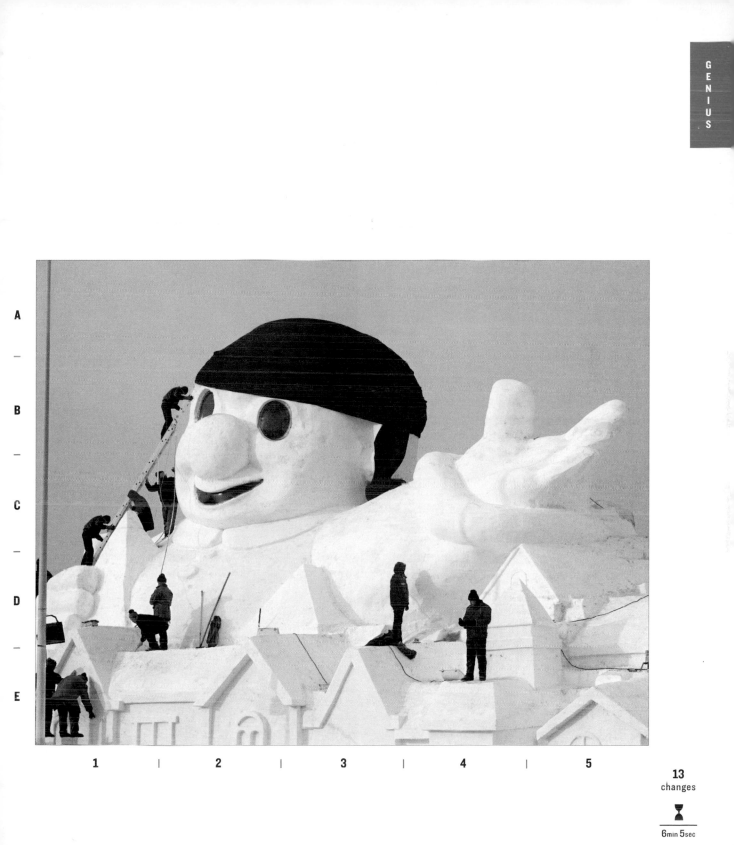

A
—
B
—
C
—
D
—
E

1   2   3   4   5

13
changes

⧖

6min 5sec

Answers
on page 142

KEEP SCORE ★ ❏ ❏ ❏ ❏ ❏ ❏ ❏ ❏ ❏ ❏ ❏ ❏ ❏

Not Another Monkey Doll

As they say in baseball: Wait till next year

TOM ERVIN/GETTY

17
changes
- - - - - - - - -
KEEP
SCORE

6min 15sec

Answers
on page 142

Stocking Stuffing

A mischievous imp changed everything when no one was looking

A
—
B
—
C
—
D
—
E

1   2   3   4   5

21
changes

⧗

7min 5sec

Answers
on page 143

KEEP SCORE ★ ❑

ICS[ ]

These puzzles were
specially created with
memorable photos
from the LIFE archives.

End of the Line

About to take a tumble in the snow,
these holiday skiers know it's all in good fun

RALPH MORSE/LIFE

A

B

C

D

E

1   2   3   4   5

9
changes

- - - - - - - - -

KEEP
SCORE

❏
❏
❏
❏
❏
❏
❏
❏
❏

⏳

3min 25sec

Answers
on page 143

A Gentle Reminder

We all need to remember that giving is better than receiving

PETER STACKPOLE/LIFE

A

–

B

–

C

–

D

–

E

1   2   3   4   5

7
changes

KEEP
SCORE

⏳

3min 5sec

Answers
on page 143

The Ties That Bind

The family that decorates together . . . decorates together

GEORGE SILK/LIFE

6
changes

- - - - - - - - -

KEEP
SCORE

☐
☐
☐
☐
☐
☐

⧗

2min 50sec

Answers
on page 143

A

B

C

D

E

1   2   3   4   5

Guarding the Sweets

As a small town gets ready for Thanksgiving,
this boy has chosen his spot very carefully

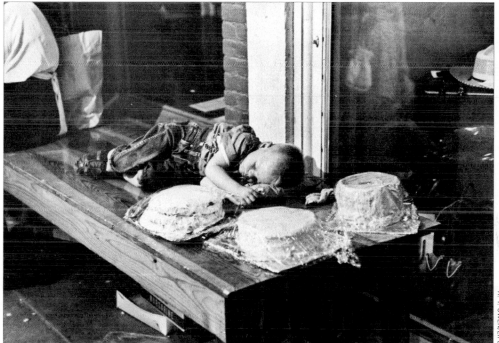

A. Y. OWEN/LIFE

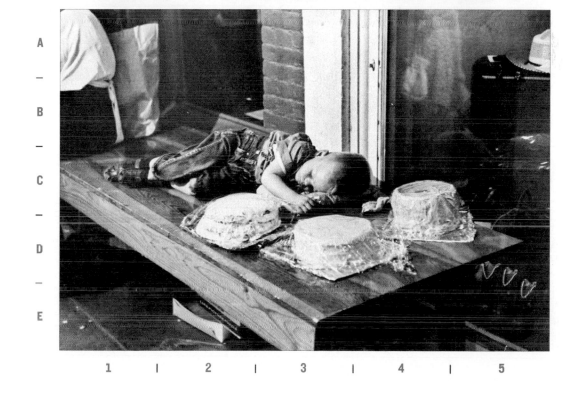

A
—
B
—
C
—
D
—
E

1 | 2 | 3 | 4 | 5

9
changes

KEEP
SCORE

⌛
3min 55sec

Answers
on page 143

Ready to Roll

It looks like someone's getting wheelies

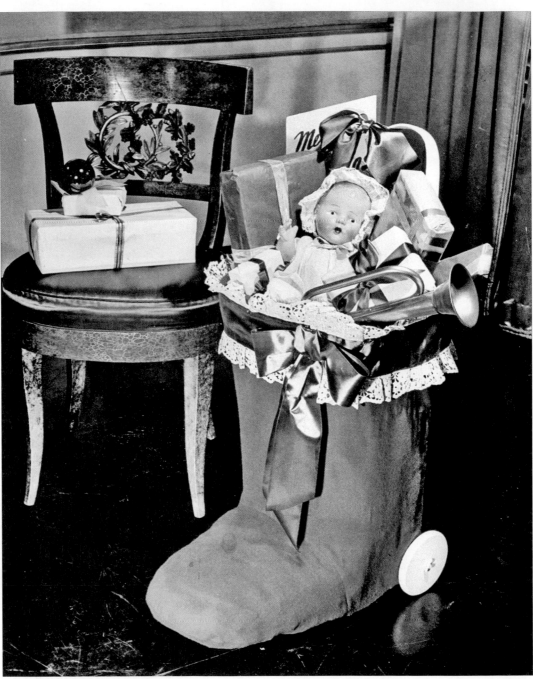

A

B

C

D

E

1   2   3   4   5

7
changes
- - - - - - - - -
KEEP
SCORE

❏
❏
❏
❏
❏
❏
❏

⧗

3min 35sec

Answers
on page 143

Tremendous Teddy

He doesn't look dangerous, does he?
Just give him a bear hug.

RALPH MORSE/LIFE

A — B — C — D — E

1 | 2 | 3 | 4 | 5

KEEP SCORE ★ ❏ ❏ ❏ ❏ ❏ ❏ ❏ ❏ ❏ ❏

10
changes

⧗
3min 50sec

Answers
on page 143

Holiday Stopping

Some things remain the same,
and last-minute shopping has never been fun

ANDREAS FEININGER/LIFE

A
–
B
–
C
–
D
–
E

1 2 3 4 5

8 changes

KEEP SCORE
❏ ❏
❏ ❏
❏ ❏
❏ ❏

⧗
5min 15sec

Answers on page 143

Heavy Traffic

When these guys are on the march, they've got the right-of-way

11
changes

KEEP
SCORE

⏳
4min 55sec

Answers
on page 143

ANSWERS

Finished already? Let's see how you did.

[INTRODUCTION]

Page 3:A Night of Miracles No. 1 (B2): He's almost a foot taller with his crown. Nos. 2 and 3 (B3): While her innocence makes her halo float, this camel wags his tongue. No. 4 (C2): He's Mister Greensleeves. No. 5 (D1): The ribbon's been cut. No. 6 (D4 to D5): The camel's let his hem down. No. 7 (D5 to E5): Beaver alert! This walking stick's been nibbled away. No. 8 (E1): She has been rehearsing for so long that she's gained six inches. No. 9 (E3): Either the logs are getting longer or the snow is melting.

[NOVICE]

Page 8:Elf Incoming No. 1 (B2): Santa's pom-pom has turned red in the slipstream. No. 2 (B3): The wing has had a quick paint job. No. 3 (B4 to C4): They opened the plane door after Santa bolted. No. 4 (B5): The reindeer's antler is still growing. No. 5 (D3): Santa has lost a boot. No. 6 (D4): The wheel can no longer strut its stuff. No. 7 (D5): Watch out for the mutant . . . reindeer.

Page 10:Ring Around the Snowman No. 1 (A2): Somehow an extra branch has grown on a painted tree. No. 2 (A3 to B3): He's flipped his head. Now, why can't we do that? No. 3 (B1): She's switched to a green cap. No. 4 (B3): Something's making him frown. No. 5 (B4): She has lost her curl. No. 6 (B4 to B5): You can tell by the eyes, he has finally got her interest. No. 7 (C2): The orange diamonds on her sweater are now purple. No. 8 (C3): The cuff on her sweater is getting longer. No. 9 (E4): She has lifted her boot out of the snow.

Page 12:The Scent of Winter No. 1 (B3 to B4): The mountaintop has reversed itself. No. 2 (B4): The moon is gone. No. 3 (B5): This peak is uplifting. No. 4 (C1): An extra aspen has popped up on the shore. No. 5 (D3 to D4): The mountain's reflection has been compressed. Nos. 6 and 7 (D3): The antler is longer, but the snout is shorter. No. 8 (E3): He's hiding a front leg.

Page 14:Fire Down Under No. 1 (A1 to A2): A shell burst is blushing pink. No. 2 (D1 to E1): One yellow bridge tower is now bathed in pink. No. 3 (D4 to D5): This tower has turned blue. No. 4 (D5): An explosion has faded away. No. 5 (E1): The sailors seem content to let the boat drift downstream. No. 6 (E5): His shirttail has drooped.

Page 16:Ho! Ho! Aloha! No. 1 (B4): The bell has rung its last. No. 2 (B5 to C5): There's a housing boom going up and up. No. 3 (C1): The life preserver must be saving someone somewhere else. No. 4 (C3 to D3): Watch out! Snorkelers are moving into the area. Nos. 5 and 6 (C4): This cool Santa has grown a fluffler cuff and donned neat shades. No. 7 (D2): His blue swimming trunks are now maroon.

Page 18:Hay There! No. 1 (C3): He's dropped his rake and hasn't even noticed. No. 2 (C3 to D3): His hat has been reversed. No. 3 (D1): There's extra hay in this part of the field. Maybe it fell off. Nos. 4 and 5 (D4): The draft horse is getting darker, while the wooden shaft is growing longer. No. 6 (D5): This pile of hay must be on the wagon now.

Page 20:Pining for Christmas No. 1 (A1 to E1): There's a steady snowfall now. Nos. 2 and 3 (C1): The tree has dropped an c and this hat can't possibly fit her. No. 4 (C4): The horse looks more festive with a green ribbon. No. 5 (C5): These horses have curiously large heads. No. 6 (E1 to E5): Soon there will be enough snow on the ground for a snowball fight.

Page 22:North Pole Pooches No. 1 (A3): My, what a blue house that is. No. 2 (A4): He has swapped noses with the little terrier. No. 3 (A4 to B4): And he's stretching his neck to get a better look at something. No. 4 (B1 to B2): Some of the brush has been cleared away. No. 5 (D2): He won those goggles in a poker game. No. 6 (C4): One of the tie strings on this cape has been stretched out. No. 7 (E2): The paw is a little darker now. No. 8 (E4): This doggie's paw looks a little swollen and tender.

Page 23:On Holiday No. 1 (B3 to D3): This nervous ex-smoker keeps turning around and around. No. 2 (B4): She loves her new helmet. No. 3 (C1 to D1): Blue is the new red. No. 4 (C2 to D2): The glove is going to fall as soon as it realizes the ski pole is missing. No. 5 (C4 to D4): Her headband is now green. No. 6 (E1): All the skiing has caused a growth spurt in her legs. No. 7 (E2): O.K., who took the skis?

Page 24:Santa's Not-So-Little Helpers No. 1 (A3): Don't look now, but the landing gear has been wheeled away. No. 2 (A3 to A4): Santa's got his own plane. No. 3 (A5): The tail is now true blue. No. 4 (B1): Security has driven off. No. 5 (B4 to B5): This car has moved up. No. 6 (E1): This jolly old gent almost missed his plane. No. 7 (E2): That's a big old boot, isn't it? No. 8 (E4): We told you, blue is the new red. No. 9 (E5): There's always somebody who has to be different.

Page 26: Silent Night No. 1 (A3 to B3): The steeple is getting steeper. No. 2 (A4 to A5): Even in winter the branch keeps growing. Nos. 3 and 4 (B1): The inn has added another room, while just below it, a window has cut through a branch. No. 5 (B1 to B2): The eave has quite a hangover. No. 6 (B2): The Christmas tree is imitating the steeple. No. 7 (C4): Someone's planted another tree. No. 8 (D3): The railing has an extra post. No. 9 (D4): The column in the center of the bridge is longer.

Page 28: Looking for a Hiding Place No. 1 (A1): Stop annoying the tom by pulling on his tail feathers! No. 2 (A5): Insects have been chewing on the leaf. No. 3 (B2): He's switched his eye makeup to green. No. 4 (B4): She's looking nervously around. No. 5 (C3 to D3): He has a low-riding wattle. No. 6 (D1 to E3): The termites are doing a number on this log. No. 7 (E5): Her tail shortens up when she's scared.

Page 29: A Wish and a Prayer No. 1 (C2 to C3): The golden circle on the daughter's top is migrating south. Nos. 2 and 3 (D1): The decorations on Mom's clothing keep changing. No. 4 (D3 to D4): This candle gets longer as it burns. No. 5 (E1): Her clothes have dropped a dot. No. 6 (E2): Chameleon candles can change colors as they burn. No. 7 (E2 to E3): Mom's hand is in front of the candle. No. 8 (E4): The flame has ditched its candle for a solo act. No. 9 (E5): Dad's clothing is getting in on the act.

Page 30: Rock Center Serenade No. 1 (A1): Yep, the building is a high-rise. No. 2 (A3 to B3): The mayor wanted a taller tree. No. 3 (B2): Someone's working late. No. 4 (B4): We've always wanted to see our name in lights. No. 5 (E1): The gate is open. No. 6 (E2): Those stars you're seeing really are there. No. 7 (E3): Prometheus gets so excited at Christmas that he can't stop spinning. No. 8 (E4 to E5): The canopy is now a delightful shade of salmon.

Page 32: Fan-tastic Festivities No. 1 (A3 to A4): It must be a fan of lavender. No. 2 (A5 to B5): Be careful of the wide-load sliding door. No. 3 (B2): Her shoulder is so sharp, it's cut the shaft in half. No. 4 (B3): With her new hairdo, she's six inches taller. No. 5 (C3): The beard wiggles and waggles. No. 6 (C4 to D5): In a note of unfelicitous disharmony, the pole of this fan is now blue. No. 7 (E1 to E2): She's got happy feet. No. 8 (E3): With imperial majesty, he literally floats across the ground.

Page 34: Winter Wonderland In photo No. 2 an avalanche has swept away the little church.

Page 35: Wet Christmas One of these scuba divers has lost his hat in photo No. 6.

Page 36: Northward Ho! No. 1 (A3 to B3): The sky is putting on quite a light show. No. 2 (A5): They haven't even noticed that Santa's on his way. No. 3 (B1): The moon must have set. Nos. 4 and 5 (B5): How can you lose a mountain? Ask the swiveling treetop, maybe it's seen it. No. 6 (C1): A skier has emerged from the woods. No. 7 (D3): She has turned to look at him. No. 8 (D4): This guy's breaking new trail.

Page 38: Slippin' and Slidin' No. 1 (A2 to B2): The spaceship looks like it's melting. No. 2 (A4): More bricks are being added to the chimney. No. 3 (B4 to B5): Someone's turning on the lights. No. 4 (C1): As the ship gets smaller, the building gets taller. No. 5 (C1 to D1): Baby, there's a new iceboat in town. No. 6 (C2 to D2): The boat's sail is flapping in the breeze. No. 7 (D1): Someone has slid away. No. 8 (D2): The boat's frame has been extended. No. 9 (D4): This lazy skier is drifting along. No. 10 (D5): His brother has inched into view.

Page 40: New Year's Wishes

3	1
2	4

Page 41: Cold War

2	4
1	3

Page 42: Brought to You by the Letter *B* No. 1 (A4 to B4): His tail's been nailed. Anyone have a patch kit? No. 2 (B1 to C1): One window light goes out and another comes on. No. 3 (B2 to B3): Look at Big Bird's collar and remember: Blue is the new red. No. 4 (B5 to C5): Two windows are now one. No. 5 (D1 to E1): This guy thinks he's the leader of the pack. No. 6 (D2): Beaks keep growing as birds get older. No. 7 (D3 to E3): He must be marching to the beat of a different drummer. No. 8 (D3): Floating in the air makes the letter *A* a little green. No. 9 (D4 to D5): Is this cap regulation color?

[MASTER]

Page 46: Riding the Rails No. 1 (A3 to B3): The coat hanger has vanished. No. 2 (A5 to B5): The handle turns. No. 3 (B2 to D5): It's a wacky mirror terrain outside the window. No. 4 (B3): The plane is really cruising along. No. 5 (C5 to D5): This lonely reindeer is pressing his nose up against the window. No. 6 (C4): Santa's made the news. No. 7 (E4): The eyeglass case is a little bloated. No. 8 (D5): Now he has a handle on that bell. No. 9 (E3): He's slipped the ring onto another finger.

Page 48: Apple Pie-to-Be No. 1 (B2 to B3): The ladder has one rung less. No. 2 (B3): The cart's handle is lopsided. No. 3 (C4): A tree has been relocated. No. 4 (C5 to D5): Oh, it's a surprise basket. No. 5 (D1 to D2): The handle has shrunk. No. 6 (D2): This green apple has lost its way. No. 7 (D3): And so has the red one.

Page 50: Who Let the Hounds Out? There are more barks coming from photo No. 3.

Page 51: Let Sleeping Bears Lie In photo No. 2, the bear has a bigger sniffer.

Page 52: The Holidays Make Us Sappy No. 1 (A1 to B1): His cap gives new meaning to "full to the brim." No. 2 (A3): Who chopped down the sapling? No. 3 (B2 to C2): His sleeve is stripier. No. 4 (B4 to B5): The harness has lost a strap. Nos. 5 and 6 (D1 to E1): All the maple syrup has warped the bucket and lengthened a branch. No. 7 (D2): The patch has been patched. No. 8 (D5): The pony has restless hoof syndrome. No. 9 (E3): He's making a style statement with this sock.

Page 54: Window-Shopping No. 1 (A3): Liberty's crown is getting pointier. No. 2 (A4): Gonzo has a really, really big salute. No. 3 (A5): Beaker is giving Carrot Top's hair a run for its money. No. 4 (D1 to C1): The officer's hat is fat. Nos. 5 and 6 (B3): The flagpole has been shortened and Fozzie Bear has lost his cap. No. 7 (B4): Kermit's kind of shy. No. 8 (B5): Talk about bug-eyed! No. 9 (C4): Would someone let Santa out of the statue? No. 10 (D4 to E4): Miss Liberty's eye is looking a little lazy.

Page 55: Capital Decorations No. 1 (A4): The President asked for a more patriotic star. No. 2 (A5): The moon is on a diet. No. 3 (B2): A tree grows at the White House. No. 4 (B4 to C4): Call an electrician! The Christmas tree lights are going out. No. 5 (C1): The flag blows with the breeze. No. 6 (D1): They must be doing repair work on the columns. No. 7 (D3): A streetlight went dark. No. 8 (E2): This bush is a little blue.

Page 56: Everything Old Is New Again No. 1 (A3): This figurine is sidling away while she can. No. 2 (B2): The hat buckle is huge. No. 3 (B2): When the boy blushes, it's his hair that turns red. No. 4 (B4 to B5): Why is Dad wearing a headdress? No. 5 (C2): It's driving Mom to drink. No. 6 (D2 to D5): Did someone spill cranberry sauce on the stripe? No. 7 (D4 to E4): The table doesn't have a leg to stand on.

Page 58: Baby, It's Cold Outside No. 1 (B1): The traffic light is splitting up. No. 2 (B3 to B4): The sign is even more spectacular now that it's blue. No. 3 (C1 to D1): Another traffic light may have blown away. No. 4 (C3 to D3): Have you checked out our new Puzzle Shop? No. 5 (C5): This is the new home of the Future Shop. No. 6 (D2): It's stop, go, and slow down all at the same time. Nos. 7 and 8 (D5): Her cap is now green, which has flipped out the traffic sign. No. 9 (E2): The taxi is in wheel trouble. No. 10 (E3): It's also lost its light.

Page 60: Sleigh to Go No. 1 (B1 to C1): They're keeping their hands warm in their pockets. No. 2 (B2): The cold has turned his cap purple. No. 3 (C1): This lady is cold enough to put her glove on. No. 4 (C2): The accordionist has learned a new chord. No. 5 (C2 to C3): The horses are stretching the driver's arms out. No. 6 (C3 to D3): A harness strap is broken. No. 7 (C5): He has opened his mouth to gulp more air. No. 8 (D1): The sleigh's runners are longer. Nos. 9 and 10 (D2): The sleigh is also missing a strut and some leaves from the decorations. Nos. 11 and 12 (D5): Not only has the middle horse lost his leg wrapping, he's about to trip another horse.

Page 62: Auld Lang Syne No. 1 (A1 to A2): This explosion has gone green. No. 2 (A4): Another shell has just burst. No. 3 (B3): The taller tower gives better TV reception. No. 4 (D2): We've rented this sign for the night. Nos. 5 and 6 (C4 to D4): They had a special on signs, so we added these two as well. No. 7 (E2): One boat is floating with the current. No. 8 (E5): Another has drifted out of view.

Page 64: Early to Rise No. 1 (B4): The chandelier has an unusual replacement bulb. No. 2 (B5): Santa has added a bauble to the tree. No. 3 (C1): The lampshade is dwindling. No. 4 (C5): The ribbon is blue. No. 5 (D1): This must be a book about levitation. Nos. 6 and 7 (D2): Someone's been embroidering the sock and nipping on the wine. No. 8 (E2 to E3): Remember what we said about blue being the new red? Never mind. No. 9 (D3): The fireplace is burning through the supply of logs. No. 10 (E1): A book is hiding under the chair. No. 11 (E4): The present has an extra bow.

Page 66: Camel Rides: Only One Ruble No. 1 (A2): His hat is puffier. No. 2 (B1): She loves her new green coat. No. 3 (B2): Each Christmas her braid gets a bit longer. Nos. 4 and 5 (B3): Someone's giving us a royal wave, and the boy's cap is blue. No. 6 (C1): The board is extending off the wagon. No. 7 (C1 to D3): Remember the musical *Paint Your Wagon*? No. 8 (C3): The driver's dropped one of the reins. No. 9 (D1 to D2): Part of the wagon bed is missing. No. 10 (D5 to E5): The camel is putting his best foot forward.

Page 68: The Russians Are Coming The doll in photo No. 2 is a little blue.

Page 69: Fa-La-La-La-La! All the hats are now the same color in photo No. 6.

Page 70: Dancing for Snowflakes No. 1 (A5): A frond is no more. No. 2 (B3): The palm is more symmetrical now. No. 3 (B3 to B4): Uh-oh, Diamond Head is bulging upward. No. 4 (C2): Part of the trunk must be transparent. No. 5 (C5 to D5): The sail has red stripes. No. 6 (D1): He's wearing a pink T-shirt. No. 7 (D2): Her skirt hangs low. No. 8 (D3): One of these girls lost the lei on her head. No. 9 (D5): The lady on the right has donned Santa's cap. No. 10 (E1): Santa decided that swimming in his clothes isn't a good idea and he's gone to towel off. No. 11 (E3 to E4): We've left our mark on the pool. No. 12 (E4): There's an extra rattle gourd, if anyone wants to play.

Page 72: It's a Wrap No. 1 (A1 to B1): The gold ribbon has been pulled out of shape. No. 2 (A2 to A3): An ornament has color-shifted. No. 3 (B4): So has this one. Nos. 4 and 5 (B5): One of these baubles is sagging. In case it falls, here's an extra ball for the tree. No. 6 (C1 to C2): Where did this stocking come from? Nos. 7 and 8 (C3): Who tore the ribbon off the present? Teddy's smiling—maybe it was him. No. 9 (D3): The snowman's nose is green. No. 10 (D5 to E5): The gold foil is blue. No. 11 (E4): The cap is all green.

Page 74: Monkey Shines Nos. 1 and 2 (B1): Not only is the building taller, it's also turned its top around. No. 3 (B2 to C2): This building is going up as well. No. 4 (B2 to B3): They've added more apartments to this one. Nos. 5 and 6 (B4): The monkey has put on a blue mask and pulled his tie in front. No. 7 (B5): He has a longer pole now, too. No. 8 (C5): How many watts is this bulb? Nos. 9 and 10 (D2): This is now a stretch barge, and one of its tires is in front of the tarp. No. 11 (D3): The canopy is solid red—stripes are so wishy-washy. No. 12 (D5): And yellow makes a stronger statement than pink.

Page 76: Central Cooling

3	5
6	1
2	4

Page 77: The Brothers Claus

5	4
2	1
3	6

Page 78: All Tied Down Nos. 1 and 2 (A5): Not only is this balloon moving away, it's also changing color. No. 3 (B2 to C1): Spidey's arm has more webbing. No. 4 (B4 to C4): He's also got a purple spot between his eyes. No. 5 (B5): Someone's awake and turning lights on in the apartment. No. 6 (C2): A distant spotlight has gone out. No. 7 (C3 to D3): One of the mooring lines has snapped. No. 8 (C5 to D5): The red has spread on his arm. No. 9 (D1): Stop adding helium! His finger is going to pop. No. 10 (E4): The ballast bag went green.

[EXPERT]

Page 82: The Glow of the Season No. 1 (A2): A branch hangs low. No. 2 (A4): The chimney's on the move. No. 3 (B1): A bracket has fallen off the eave. No. 4 (B2): The drainpipe has turned around. No. 5 (B2 to C3): The homeowners wanted blue lights for this wreath. No. 6 (B3): More glass lets in more light. No. 7 (B4 to D5): Bare tree, bright lights look nice. No. 8 (C1): The eave has been supersized. Nos. 9 and 10 (C2 to D3): The new wreath lights are pretty, but will the shutters still close? No. 11 (D3): The door just got woodier. No. 12 (D5): The tree is not as close as it looked.

Page 84: Caught Napping No. 1 (A3): The red bow is a lefty. No. 2 (A5): The top door panels are missing, but the middle ones have stretched. No. 3 (B2): One ornament looks a little large for the tree. No. 4 (B2 to B3): Candlelight casts a lovely glow. No. 5 (B3 to C3): The stocking is so full, it's drooping. No. 6 (B4): A hopeful child added a last-minute stocking. No. 7 (C1): There's supposed to be less milk, not more. No. 8 (C4): This fireplace is a double-wide. No. 9 (C4 to D5): It's possible the boy is color-blind. No. 10 (C5): What happened to the keyhole? No. 11 (D1): The beach ball is playing games with its stripes. No. 12 (D2): Does Santa know that the chair is missing a leg? No. 13 (D3): Santa lost some of his heel, so his feet seem to be floating above the rug. Maybe that's how the sleigh works. No. 14 (E2 to E3): The rug is larger than it first looked.

Page 86: A Bumpkin With Pumpkins No. 1 (B1): The chain has slipped over the pedal. No. 2 (B2): Has the scarecrow been telling lies? No. 3 (B3): The wheel is missing some spokes. Nos. 4 and 5 (B5): Not only has this pumpkin started to bloat, someone's been carving it. No. 6 (C2 to C3): His sleeve is not as plaid as it was. No. 7 (C4): The gourd is engorged. No. 8 (C5): The top of the post made the termites happy. No. 9 (D1): The sleepy kitty is named Zacky. No. 10 (D3 to D4): The rear fender is blue. No. 11 (E3): The pumpkin's lost its stem. No. 12 (E4 to E5): More leaves are falling.

Page 88: Teach Your Children Well Nos. 1 and 2 (B2): One good look at her new lipstick has started the candlewick spinning. Nos. 3 and 4 (B3): Her scrunchies are blue, and her pigtail is longer. Nos. 5 and 6 (B4): His yarmulke is now a handsome magenta, and her pearl earring needs a reappraisal. No. 7 (B5): The windows have more—but smaller—panes. No. 8 (D1): The matchbox holds longer matches now. No. 9 (D2): Mom has removed her watch. No. 10 (D3): She has pushed her bracelet up her arm. No. 11 (E1 to E2): The base of the menorah has been downsized.

Page 90: Dicey Business No. 1 (A1): A replacement die is waiting in the wings. No. 2 (A2): His nose gives him quite a striking pose. Nos. 3 and 4 (A3): The berries are multiplying, which sent the box into a purple rage. No. 5 (B2): Christmas seems to have misplaced its C. No. 6 (B4): The red ribbon has a longer point. No. 7 (B5): The gold fabric has a broader perspective. No. 8 (D2): The G has toppled over. Nos. 9 and 10 (D3): Don't bet on this game. The dice are crooked. No. 11 (D4 to E5): This ribbon blues us away. No. 12 (E3): Vermont Avenue is a little too pricey for our taste.

Page 92: That Lived-In Look Nos. 1 and 2 (A1): The rosy lampshades are now three. No. 3 (A3): The red kerchief took a powder. No. 4 (A5): This kerchief is bluish. No. 5 (B4): It's a candle meant for giants, or at least tall folks. No. 6 (C4): The candleholder is being erased from existence. No. 7 (D4): An apple a day . . . No. 8 (D5): Danger Vase lives life on the edge. No. 9 (E3 to E4): The chair favors the natural look.

Page 93: Santa's Mail Room No. 1 (A2 to B2): The two sides of the window have achieved unity. No. 2 (A3): Santa's hat has peaked. No. 3 (A4): The stars are out tonight—at least on this blackboard. No. 4 (B4): Blackboard Santa is feeling green. No. 5 (C3): Her beard needs a trim. No. 6 (C3 to C4): Someone's started to rewrite the letter. No. 7 (C5): The balloon is in the pink. No. 8 (D1 to E1): She's keeping her arm to herself.

Page 94: Dive, Dive, Dive No. 1 (A3 to A4): The flag goes up. No. 2 (A4 to A5): So does the light. No. 3 (B4): The sub's captain lost his pockets. No. 4 (C2 to C3): Santa has changed his gloves. No. 5 (C4): The sub's sail has lost a vent. Nos. 6 and 7 (C5): While the running light changed its color, two sailors may have gone overboard. No. 8 (D2 to D3): Santa's wet robe has sagged. No. 9 (D4 to D5): As the metal platform shrank, this sailor got leggier. No. 10 (E1 to E5): Either the water level is dropping or the sub is floating higher. No. 11 (E2): The water gauge has been extended.

Page 96: In Search of Santa's Workshop No. 1 (A1 to A5): The aurora is flickering backward and forward. No. 2 (C5): One more candle won't change much in this darkness. No. 3 (D2): The blanket has been redesigned. No. 4 (D2 to E2): The hamper has lost its frame. Nos. 5 and 6 (D3): A pot is missing but a snowshoe has gained a Star of David. No. 7 (D4): The sled is green. No. 8 (D5): A snowshoe is sinking deeper into the snow. No. 9 (E1): Is that Santa sneaking away? No. 10 (E4): Another pot has been set down near the lantern.

Page 98: The North Wind Blows In photo No. 3, two horses are trying to graze.

Page 99: Berried Alive The side flanges on the harvester are longer in photo No. 4.

Page 100: Gabriel, Blow Your Horn! No. 1 (A4): The steeple has boarded up a window. No. 2 (B1): Two windows have traded places. Nos. 3, 4, and 5 (B2): One roof has gone crimson, five chimneys have shrunk, and a building has gained a dormer. No. 6 (C1): The drummer's put on a high hat. No. 7 (C2): This sheet music holds more notes on each page. No. 8 (C2 to D2): The rail's gone wide. No. 9 (C3): The tuba has a golden bell. No. 10 (D3): Those are long leggings. No. 11 (D4): The slide has slid. No. 12 (E4): Those cobblestones are fat.

Page 101: Please Don't Eat the Houses
No. 1 (A2 to B2): The curtains are closing.
No. 2 (A3): The red stocking stands out more.
No. 3 (B1): Blondie needs a haircut. No. 4 (B2 to B3): He's got a secret—he just had a trim.
No. 5 (B4 to C4): Where did the candy cane come from? No. 6 (B5 to C5): The strap has snapped. No. 7 (C4 to D4): His shirt should have been washed in cold water. No. 8 (C5): The green from the stocking has jumped onto the sleeve. No. 9 (D4): If you like wintergreen, this is the mint for you. No. 10 (E1): The plate of cookies is skidding across the table. No. 11 (E2): Did someone eat the gingerbread man?

Page 102: It's Called Skijoring No. 1 (A1): The horse's new name is Patches. No. 2 (A3): His ears have pricked up. No. 3 (B1): The blue rail is no more. Nos. 4 and 5 (B3): His headband is blue, and the strap went *kaboom*. No. 6 (B4 to B5): This helmet has blanched. No. 7 (B5): Those are cowardly goggles. No. 8 (C1): The chest strap has green trimming. No. 9 (C4 to D4): His green pants go better with the rest of his outfit . No. 10 (C4 to C5): He hasn't noticed that he's lost his watch. No. 11 (C5 to D5): The stripe has been stripped out. No. 12 (D2): His leg bands are now red. No. 13 (D4): A hoof has gone *poof*. No. 14 (D5): This pant leg could trip him up. No. 15 (E2): And this hoof is enormous. No. 16 (E4): With skis, apparently size does matter.

[GENIUS]

Page 106: Look! It's Sandy Claus Nos. 1 and 2 (A2): A bird is on the wing, and the curtains are open. No. 3 (C1): The lamp has no visible means of support. Nos. 4 and 5 (C2): Santa's lost his pom-pom, and the markings on his board are retreating. No. 6 (C3 to C4): We like seeing the word LIFE in red. No. 7 (D1 to E1): Someone has a twin. No. 8 (D1): A hand has lifted. No. 9 (D2): The wet suit has a long arm. Nos. 10 and 11 (D3): His pants have been let down, and a red shirt's gone blue. No. 12 (D4): She's lost her yellow wristband. No. 13 (D4 to D5): This board's stripe has worn away. No. 14 (E5): Here's the soccer ball you lost.

Page 108: Urban Snowscape No. 1 (A1): The rooftop is a little steeper. No. 2 (C3 to C4): The branches are creeping across the road. No. 3 (D1): The tree is growing through the fire escape. No. 4 (D5): A window has been pulled upward like taffy. No. 5 (E2): The SUV must have been sideswiped, because it's lost a mirror. No. 6 (E2 to E3): These three have staggered their way forward. Nos. 7, 8, and 9 (E3): While the guy way down the street keeps trying to get across, not only has this couple made good time, they've also traded places. No. 10 (E4 to E5): Someone's running their car battery down.

Page 110: Make Like a Nutcracker No. 1 (A1): His hat has green trim now. No. 2 (A3): The words are translating themselves into Russian. Nos. 3 and 4 (A5): The bayonet is floating up, and the hat is getting larger. No. 5 (B1 to C1): He's popped a button off his uniform.

No. 6 (B2): Those are a lot of nails in the sole of his boot. Nos. 7 and 8 (B3): His sleeve has an extra stripe and the letter A is floating upside down. No. 9 (B4): His boot is shrinking. No. 10 (C5): They've gained a musician. No. 11 (D2): This boot rides high. No. 12 (E5): His nickname is Big Toes.

Page 111: Pudding No. 1 (A1 to B1): The beads are bleaching fast. No. 2 (A3): The ribbon can wrap a bigger package. No. 3 (B2): The holly leaf can't be growing, can it? No. 4 (B5): Two boxes are better than one. Nos. 5 and 6 (C1 to D2): The Christmas ball has lost its hanger and developed bands of purple. No. 7 (C5): The lid has gained a center decoration. No. 8 (D3): The knife handle has lengthened. No. 9 (D4): A flower hangs over the card. No. 10 (E2): The postcard is experiencing a sudden attack of the clones. No. 11 (E3): A flower grows on paper. No. 12 (E3): This card needs a good copy editor. No. 13 (E4): The ribbon has been cut.

Page 112: Candle Power No. 1 (A3): The bauble is the color purple. No. 2 (A4): The tree has gained an extra ornament. No. 3 (B1): The andiron is expanding. No. 4 (B2): The angel has lost her base of support. No. 5 (B4): This tiny tree's tiny ball has gone from purple to red. No. 6 (B5): The candle has been renewed. No. 7 (C2 to D2): Better recount the windows on the dollhouse. Nos. 8 and 9 (C4): A tree floats on Christmas, and the drawer has lost a knob. No. 10 (C4 to D4): The shelf is too big for its bureau. No. 11 (D2): The ribbon's reflection has vanished. No. 12 (D3 to E3): The present is larger than it was. No. 13 (D4): The handle has slipped. No. 14 (E1 to E2): The wooden box stands tall. No. 15 (E3): The rug has lost some of its design. Nos. 16 and 17 (E5): The new candle hides a missing leg.

Page 114: Frosty's Beauticians No. 1 (B1): The ladder is missing two slots. Nos. 2 and 3 (B2): He's climbing high, and the eye has a bigger window on the world. No. 4 (B4): He's got a big cold thumb. No. 5 (C1): Is this a new parka? Nos. 6 and 7 (D2): His cap is red with body heat, while the handle has elongated. No. 8 (D3): He's been turned around. No. 9 (D4 to E4): What kind of people are shadowless? Nos. 10, 11, and 12 (E1): The parka is green with fear because the platform has disappeared, and the scraper is behind the roof. No. 13 (E3): A snow window has been iced away.

Page 116: Not Another Monkey Doll
No. 1 (A4): This is what happens with too much hair mousse. No. 2 (B4): That's a pretty chimp earring. No. 3 (B5): The rope floats. No. 4 (C1 to C2): The torn cardboard has been mended.
No. 5 (C2): A flap has been cut away. No. 6 (C5): The stuffed animal has lost a spot. No. 7 (C5 to D5): He's also gaining weight. No. 8 (D1): The wrapping paper is starrier. No. 9 (D5): The stuffed animal must like being upside down, because he's smiling. No. 10 (D5 to E5): The towel is in the pink. No. 11 (E1): A snowman's doing cartwheels. No. 12 (E3): His arm

reaches down. Nos. 13 and 14 (E4): Smart chimp. He's traded the stump for a candy cane. Nos. 15, 16, and 17 (E5): One present has been taken away, but don't worry, another has been added; and by the way, who dropped the cookie?

Page 118: Stocking Stuffing Nos. 1 and 2 (A1): The wood has been depaneled, and there's a new candle in town. No. 3 (A2): Let there be light. No. 4 (A3 to B3): The stocking cuff has become turquoise. No. 5 (A3 to A4): A pinecone has been squirreled away. No. 6 (B3): A moon is snuggling up to the top of the stocking. No. 7 (B4): His sleep cap is trailing behind. No. 8 (B5): The holly leaves are sliding down. Nos. 9, 10, and 11 (C1): The costume is more gilded, the stocking is longer, and the poker is shorter. Nos. 12 and 13 (C2): The angel has a longer gown, and the log rides high. No. 14 (C3): The metal frame is screwed tighter now. No. 15 (C3 to E3): The fire curtain has been pulled out. No. 16 (C4): These holly leaves have jumped stockings. No. 17 (D5): The stonework has been repaired. No. 18 (E2): If you could understand mousesqueak, he might be saying, "More popcorn, please." No. 19 (E2 to E3): Now who's been nibbling on the popcorn? No. 20 (E3): The handle popped from green to blue. No. 21 (E5): There's no way to get a handle on this pot.

[LIFE CLASSICS]

Page 122: End of the Line No. 1 (A2 to B2): It's so cold, one tree is now two. No. 2 (B1): But it's never too cold for kids to go sledding. No. 3 (B3 to C3): This girl looks as determined as her sister. No. 4 (B4 to C4): The skier must be downslope now. No. 5 (C1): The ski has slid forward. No. 6 (C3): He must have skier's knee. No. 7 (C4): His cap is loftier now. No. 8 (D5): Does he know the rope broke? No. 9 (E1 to E2): This ski is finally free.

Page 124: A Gentle Reminder Nos. 1 and 2 (A1): As the office light goes on, the tripod struts its stuff. No. 3 (A2 to A3): This angel is really blowing her horn. No. 4 (B3 to C4): Her chin strap snapped. No. 5 (C4): The coat buttons up tighter now. No. 6 (C5): Stonemasons have extended the wall. No. 7 (D2 to E3): She's standing in front of the tripod.

Page 126: The Ties That Bind No. 1 (A3): The fire extinguisher has a brand-new cone. No. 2 (A4): The speaker has reversed itself. No. 3 (B1): Dad's collar has darkened. No. 4 (B4 to C4): He has ditched his glasses. No. 5 (C3): She has been tugging on her sweater sleeve too much. No. 6 (D3): How can they sell no snow?

Page 127: Guarding the Sweets No. 1 (A1): The brim on this bag can be fuller now. No. 2 (A3 to B3): These are twice the bricks they were before. No. 3 (A4): Gravity is tugging the window latch lower. No. 4 (A5 to B5): The luggage has pushed the hat higher. No. 5 (C1): The boy is growing fast. No. 6 (C3 to C4): Also, he needs a haircut. No. 7 (E2): They seem to have tucked a box of our books under the table. Here's hoping they hand them out later. No. 8 (E2 to D5): The table can take a bigger load now. No. 9 (E5): The boots are multiplying.

Page 128: Ready to Roll No. 1 (A1 to A3): The chair back has been reinforced. Nos. 2 and 3 (A3 to A4): The molding must have been sold, but at least the Christmas card has been delivered. No. 4 (B5 to C5): A bigger bell helps the trumpet bray louder. No. 5 (C1 to D1): Just make sure you don't lean back in this chair. No. 6 (E1 to E2): Who knows how big the toe can grow? No. 7 (E4 to E5): It's no reflection on the wheel.

Page 130: Tremendous Teddy No. 1 (A2 to A3): The column's been truncated. No. 2 (A3 to B3): Well-loved teddy bears often lose their ears. Nos. 3 and 4 (A5): The wooden soldier wears a tall hat and the last tree rises high. No. 5 (B2): The shadows are disappearing. No. 6 (B3): His nose has been sadly diminished. No. 7 (C3): He's plucked the buttons off his sleeve. No. 8 (D1): The buggy has lost a wheel. No. 9 (D3 to E3): He's got one big foot. No. 10 (E4 to E5): And one long leg.

Page 132: Holiday Stopping No. 1 (A5): Two windows are playing leapfrog. No. 2 (C2): This street has a new name. No. 3 (C2 to C3): The lamp is bulging. No. 4 (C5): There are more police on the beat. No. 5 (D1): Santa's making a cameo appearance. No. 6 (D4): In case you didn't notice, they store cheese in this warehouse. No. 7 (E2 to E3): He may be taking his life in his hands trying to cross the street right now. No. 8 (E4): Shoppers keep pouring out onto the street. At least she's smiling.

Page 134: Heavy Traffic No. 1 (A1): The car drove off. No. 2 (A3): This restaurant must be a hop stop. No. 3 (A4): A word of advice: Don't shop for insurance here. No. 4 (A5): Quick, this store needs a sign painter. No. 5 (B1 to C1): The penguin may be out of place but at least he's well dressed. No. 6 (B5 to C5): He may have stepped inside for a soda. No. 7 (D1 to E1): This elephant cut in line. No. 8 (E1): So did this man. No. 9 (E2): This *C* has got it backward. No. 10 (E3): The elephant lifted a leg. No. 11 (E4): That's more than a 10-gallon hat.

Just One More

We couldn't leave without giving you one more holiday puzzle to enjoy.
Here, Brazilians celebrate Christmas by dancing their hearts out.

ORLANDO KISSNER/GETTY

15
changes

KEEP
SCORE

4min 50sec

ANSWERS: No. 1 (A2 to A3): **The roof points upward.** No. 2 (A5): Night comes later with the extra light. No. 3 (B3): His legging has lost its bindings. No. 4 (C1 to C2): This scarf is decidedly blue. No. 5 (C4 to D4): This scarf is a tad longer. No. 6 (D1): His T-shirt is a mellow yellow. No. 7 (E1): His leg is floating. Nos. 8 and 9 (D2): As the logs get the urge to merge, he's donned his sunglasses. No. 10 (D3): Her gold edging is edgier. No. 11 (E3): His leg is grounded. No. 12 (D5): His scarf is blue too. No. 13 (D5 to E5): They wish they had a better view. No. 14 (E1 to E2): The teardrop is bigger. No. 15 (E4): Her heel has flown.